# Hearty Vehemence Vol II

The collection of Poems straight from my heart

Navneet Agarwal

pencil

ISBN 978-93-5610-884-4

Published in India 2022 by Pencil

*A brand of*
One Point Six Technologies Pvt. Ltd.
123, Building J2, Shram Seva Premises,
Wadala Truck Terminal, Wadala (E)
Mumbai 400037, Maharashtra, INDIA
**E** connect@thepencilapp.com
**W** www.thepencilapp.com

# Author biography

Being Born in 1991 in the small hilly town of Darjeeling, I did my schooling from the St. Joseph's College, School Department, commonly called North Point. Thereafter I went to Delhi and did my graduation from Dyal Singh College, University of Delhi. First I taught Mathematics in the Assembly of God Church School, and thereafter I went back to Delhi and worked as a Maths Expert for MCR Eduservices. This made me rethink and so I did my Masters in Economics from IGNOU and then B.Ed from CRSU. I currently work with the Assembly of God Church School as their Economics Teacher.

I have had the passion for writing since a long time and started to write poems after my mother's death. I have written a few novels as well.

# CONTENTS


1. Never Hurt Someone ........ 7

2. Strange Feeling ........ 9

3. Golden Days ........ 10

4. Lost ........ 12

5. Unanswered Questions ........ 14

6. New Year Resolution ........ 16

7. Friendship ........ 18

8. Miss You ........ 20

9. Mom, I Miss You........ 22

10. I am sorry ........ 25

11. Career ........ 27

12. Hypocrisy ........ 28

13. Mixed Feeling ........ 30

14. Lies ........ 32

15. Love You ........ 34

16. Mom, God's Creation ........ 36

17. Memories ........ 38

18. Wind ........ 40

19. Caste and Reservation ........ 42

20. Changes ........ 44

22. Be Careful ........ 46

23. Good Bye ........ 48
24. It is easy ........ 50
25. Emotional Poem ........ 51
26. Smiling Face ........ 52
27. Melancholy ........ 54
28. Destiny of Life ........ 56
29. Big Dream ........ 58
30. Feeling... Let it GO!!! ........ 59
31. Introvert ........ 61
32. Path You Choose ........ 63
33. Everyone is Talented ........ 65
34. Miss You Always ........ 67
35. Live up to You ........ 69
36. Will You be There... ........ 71
37. Hope is the Mantra ........ 73
38. Enjoy Every Moment ........ 75
39. Dream of the Soul ........ 77
40. Mistakes not Repeated ........ 79
41. Life... A Teacher ........ 81
42. Unknown Cause of Feeling ........ 83
43. I Admire You ........ 86
44. Changing Friendship ........ 88
45. Plan ........ 90
46. Memory Lane ........ 92

47. Phobia....................94
48. Questions....................96
49. Be Happy....................98
50. Teaching, A Profession....................100

# 1. Never Hurt Someone

You need to control your tongue
It may act in a total different way
The words you speak may act against you
If you don't think and say

Your words can hurt someone intensely
You may not know how much it has hurt
It sometimes is unbearable
And consequences maybe too much

Some words can scratch the heart
They are so sharp that they can make a deep cut
They can be so painful indeed
And in way can heal the cut

I have been in such situation
Not once but twice
First from a person of the same age
And other one from my prize

But the thing hurts my ego
I can never forget it
I am a Scorpion indeed
I live for my egoistic belief

Religion says you should not have ego
Wars happened because of it
But every time you cannot do it away
Sometimes you have to cater to it

## 2. Strange Feeling

I have become forgetful
Now a days I am lost always
I keep on thinking about you
You are in my head always

I smile when I see you smile
I laugh at your jokes
I feel like crying when you are angry
Your sadness always pokes

While eating I think of you
While sleeping you are there in my mind
While playing you haunt me
While writing I think of you as my design

I can't stop thinking of you
You have become my breath
You are the reason I am living
I can't take without you any breath

I don't know why I think of you
I have never had such a feeling
I have a lot of explanation to it
But none matches my feeling

# 3. Golden Days

There is first time to everything
The first time I talked to openly with friends
I made them sign a bond of love
I miss those Golden days

We talked about everything
Those were talks I hardly can forget
I still remember all the bits that happened
The times I don't want to forget

The time spent inside the Twin Towers
The love that I got from every side
The bond of friendship that were built
Like the castle of cards with a brighter side

It's been years of leaving the place
All the ten years with friends
A lot have I learnt from this place
I still miss those Golden days

While parting we promised
Never to forget one another in anyways
We have kept that promise indeed
But can't remain in contact always

I do understand
We have grown up in our ways
We don't have much time for old friends
But still I miss those Golden days

The Blue Blood which we hold
Unites us in every way
We have shared common feeling always
I know, we all miss those golden days

We didn't have any worries
We hardly thought of the future
We were guided and moulded
In a very Home like nature

I cannot forget the fields
The quadrangle assemblies in every way
Each and every teacher teaching
Those were the real Golden days

## 4. Lost

I am lost in every sense
I don't know what to do next
The path I have chosen for may not work
But that is the risk that I have to take

I have a plan in my head
Will it be successful is a big question
Will everyone approve of it
And help me in all the difficult situation

The path I have thought of
Will make me move to Ground Zero
But to start something good
You have to start it from zero

It will be quite difficult for me I know
But I don't have any other choice
The plan has to be executed
At any cost effective for the choice

I don't know whether the decision is right or wrong
Whether it will lead me to success or failure
But I know only one thing
That if I don't try now I will call myself a failure

I hope God will be there with me
Like he has always been
I will never ask for his help as I have promised
But I know he will see my dedication indeed

I hope my family with support me
In every hurdle that I have to jump
They will always help me
Through every terrain I come

I want to shine like a star
Make my own world
Make it possible for me
To do as I want to live in this world

I know many will say me
It is wrong you should not do it
You are running away from your duties
Later you will repent it

But if I listen to then
I will be at a flaw
I have to open my wings and fly
Even if I have to break nature's Law

I have to try it out once
Need to take every risk at any cost
Otherwise I will be humiliated at my own eyes
And be lost in my own thought

## 5. Unanswered Questions

The questions which are there in my mind
Can't be easily answered
There may not even be any answers
And that is totally weird

When i see fathers loving their children
I get jealous
When i see fathers caring their children
I feel jealous

The feeling of envy circulates me
When i see families as families
I am jealous
When i see families as non-enemies

I just don't understand
Why do I feel that way?
I have no answers for it
Can you try and say

I had someone who dearly loved me
And i loved her too
Why did God took you away from me
And left me without you

I miss you everyday
I think of you when they talk of their mom
I feel jealous of them
But never say a word as it may hurt some

Why is life like this?
Why does it make you lonely?
The answers will never be given
But i want them only

The answers to my question
Are difficult and impossible
There are no true answers
Which is clearly possible

# 6. New Year Resolution

Every year brings hidden joy for us
The hidden surprises are there
We want to make the beginning a great thing
And speak the news everywhere

Everyone has a special way
To celebrate this occasion
Everyone wants to enjoy themselves
And mark the memories of this celebration

We all make a stupid resolution
Which we break in a month or even a week
We have all the excuses for it
But we know that we were actually very weak

Let's make this year special
By making resolution of a different type
These may seem difficult to achieve
But at least we can try and get it right

Let's make a promise
That we will not be communal
We need to look beyond
Caste and our very own religion

We have been fighting over it
Since a millennium or more than that
Once look forward to all the religion
They all hav the same thing to say remember that

All religions spread love
Friendship and non violence is their part
The violence and enmity
Is spread to tear everyone apart

Whether it is Bible, Gita or Kuran
Same things are written in them
Maybe the style is different
They all want to say the things which are same

I know this resolution can never be achieved
It is next to possibility
We have been growing up in such a place
Where the TRP is given to religious enmity.

# 7. Friendship

Friendship is greater than any other relationship
We built it up slowly
It is very beautiful part of our life
We need to cherish it truly
Love is the very essence of it
You unconditionally love your friend indeed
This is the basic pillar of love
On which the whole relation stands deep
Trust has to be there in it
You need to blindly trust your friend
This is the strongest pillar
Once it breaks it brings the relationship to it's end
Help is what is required of it
You need to help your friend in every way
This becomes the third pillar in fact
And you need to satisfy it in every way
Depend on your friend's advice
They will never give you wrong advice
So believe is the next pillar
Which will protect the relation from every vice
The very foundation of friendship is forgiveness
Forgive your friend when they have done something wrong
If you forgive you come closer
And then the bond becomes even more strong

Respect is what makes the ceiling
Of this friendship building
Respect your friend so that they can respect you
And make a very firm building

## 8. Miss You

Time flies by so quickly
It seems like we only met yesterday
Now you have left for your future
You are gone and have parted away

The two years we spent together
Will always be remembered by me
The time we spent together
Will always be cherished by me

You will remain in my heart forever
And for that I am sure
Your time spent with me
Will remain with me for sure

We have talked in between our classes
We have shared time that cannot be described
We have talked interrupting each other's class
And talked about the things that can't be described

I will remember you always
Whenever I will click a photo
You were the one who made me click them
Whether I want to or don't want to do so

The talks about Delhi and Dyal Singh
INA and Delhi Hart
The sleeping bus trips you had
Will always remain in my heart

You are the one
Who kept Delhi alive in me
You were the one who reminded
How important was Delhi for me

You are not just a friend
You are the best one indeed
Please don't forget me anytime
If you do so it will be a hurtful thing

The place you have filled in my heart with
Will always remain empty
I will miss you everyday
When I will see your place empty

## 9. Mom, I Miss You...

I am feeling sad
Deep in my heart
I miss the time I spent with you
No one should in such way part

How could you leave me
In such a place
With such people and things
In such a difficult situation

After you have gone to heaven
There is no one left for me
I am so lonely today
That there are tears and no one can see

I have sacrificed a lot
Now I cannot sacrifice any further
I have done everything I could
But now there is a blockage which cannot be solved either

Tears are coming out of my eyes
I cannot control them in any way
I have tried everything, but nothing works
I just miss your lap to cry and lay

After you have gone, I have seen
Relationship change and fade
It seems no one is there for me
You were the only one at my aid

My reasons are lost
I am not able to console myself
I miss you mom very much
You are there in my heart always

I have tried enough to cope up
To try and live my life without you
But it seems next to possibility
As I cannot find anyone so close like you

Your teachings prohibit me
To express myself clearly to others
You have always told me
Don't burden them with your soul in their's

You told me
You will always be there to listen to me
But the problem is that
I want to say to you but you are no more with me

I am too tired
Of trying to fill your space for everyone
I want to let go of it now
But it is impossible as per my turn

I just want to run away from these duties
I want never to be found again

I want to your youngest son again
I want to be as I was before, totally insane

Life has made me break down
A numerous time
I have stood up to be strong always
But it seems not this time

I have more things to say
But my tears prohibit me
I love you mom ad always will
But it's so that I cannot express me

You have gone far, very far indeed
I just hope and wish that
If there is next birth in any way
I want to get you as my mother again.

## 10. I am sorry

If I have hurt you anytime
I am sorry
If I didn't treat you the way you should have been
I am sorry
If I didn't remember your special day
I am sorry
If I have ever taken you for granted
I am sorry
If I have fought with you for no reason
I am sorry
If I have not reciprocated your love
I am sorry
If I was not present when you needed me
I am sorry
If I did not understand your problem
I am sorry
If I have ever leaked your secrets
I am sorry
If I have not told you some of my secrets
I am sorry
If I was the cause of your sadness
I am sorry
If when you made me happy, I didn't say thank you
I am sorry
If I forgot to appreciate your help

I am sorry
If I forgot to ask you for help
I am sorry
If I said some mean things to you
I am sorry
If I could not see your inner beauty
I am sorry
The times when I could not forgive you
For that I am sorry
The times I forgot to say you sorry
I am sorry
If I forgave you in an improper way
I am sorry
If I asked for forgiveness in an inappropriate way
I am sorry

# 11. Career

Career is not easy to decide
It needs a lot of analysis
You need to know all the pros and cons
In order to complete your analysis

It involves lots of phobias
One of them being failure
The other being reputation
And still there is fear of being insecure

It also is not always correct
And is full of cliches
You may not like it always
And it may be against all your wishes

If you don't choose any
Then too it is your mistake
The whole world will be after you
And will never give you a take

So, whatever you do
Think and choose it
Otherwise your life will be hell
And you cannot blame it.

# 12. Hypocrisy

We live in the world of hypocrisy
The world where we have dual face
The country says it is developing, moving forward
But things that happen are not for that race
Parliament is not allowed to function
When they say they will support the government with all ease
All the bills stay pending and no work is done
Then onsets the playing of the blame game

University is the place for education
The place where we learn to get the knowledge
Few people put up slogans which are not good
And defame the whole system of knowledge
Politicians get involved playing the blame game
News channels for TRPs don't show the true picture of indulgence
Just throwing mud is what happens altogether
And the whole matter is made of intolerance

Our constitution says us not to discriminate
On the basis of religion, creed, colour or caste
Seats are reserved in every institute
On the basis of the lower caste
Then all the other caste who are educated

Fight to make themselves of lower caste
To get reservation
To get benefits not given to the higher caste

Religion is another issue
We say all religions are the same
They have the same learnings
But still people fight in their name
Religion becomes the best thing for defending
And it is the thing which everyone wants to defend
It is said God is the one who protects
But the priests think that God is the person they need to protect

# 13. Mixed Feeling

I don't know why am I feeling strange today
I had thought of the move much before
But still the strangeness is there in my heart
To depart from the place which was close to my heart

I want to cry
But the tears are not there
I don't know what to do next
I am confused about my steps

I want to laugh all along
Smile and make my future bright
I am not being able to do that also
And I am with the mixed feeling in fact

I am sad
As, soon I will be leaving some close one
I am happy also
As I am moving ahead to brighten up

I am sad
As soon I will not remain the thing I was
I am happy also
As I will be soon in the place where everyone desires

I am sad
As I have to leave my responsibilities behind
I am happy
That the new life will have new types of responsibilities

I am sad
As I will shatter few hopes
I am happy also
As I have done what I have longed for

I am sad
As I know keep in touch doesn’t mean anything
I am happy also
As I have to do what I have thought of

I don’t have much words here
I am being speechless now
I still have few days left here
I will render my duty well and cherish my life here

# 14. Lies

Always tell the truth
Is easier said than done
We live in the world of lies
Lies are told at every turn

We need to speak the truth I know
But circumstances don't permit always
The truth has to be sugar-coated with lie
So that it can suit all needs in every way

We are introduced to lies at our birth itself
The lies of caste, religion and fate
When we get bigger in times to come
Those lies compel to change our gate

When a child cries
It is told the biggest lie
Everything will be fine, don't worry
And then chocolates are given to match the lie

Lies are told when we grow up
Lies are told when we leave or depart
We will stay in touch is one of them
It is once said and then left as a part

We are heart broken
When someone dear dies
That person is always there watching you
Is again the biggest of all lies

Heart is broken, tears come out
When your trust is broken in love
You will find someone else in times to come
Lies again find your way there in love

One universal lie is that
When you help someone
When you are there in their har times
You will be helpful by someone in return

Lies are everywhere
Lies have built up this universe
The lies are told at every stage
But lies are forbidden in every verse

## 15. Love You

You are so beautiful
By no words can you be described
You are more beautiful than any Goddess
Who are in mythology describes

Your smile is such
It can hide all the pains
Your sadness can ruin the mood
And make the day go in vain

The blush in your cheek
No word can describe it's beauty
The depth of your eyes
Is icing on the cake for your beauty

Your long hair
Make me fall in love with you
Your beautiful lips
Make me wanting to kiss you

Your lovable face
There is no clichè in it
You are so perfectly made
There is no doubt about it

You are like an angel on Earth
Beauty itself feel insecure of you
You are here to make every girl jealous
As you can make anyone fall in love with you

I will never leave you
Whatever may come in our lives
I will stay till eternity
We will stay together even after the end of your lives.

# 16. Mom, God's Creation

Mom is the most beautiful creation of God
She is actually a God in our space
No one can actually replace her
No one can fill her space

She bears pain
In order to give birth to her child
She sacrifices everything
In order to make the life of her child

She understands everything
Even the words unspoken by her child
And she without any consideration
Loves and cares for her child

She takes care of her child
Without any wish for care in return
She is always kind to her child
Even if she gets unkindness in return

She is that treasure
Which needs to be cherished all the time
You need to show her your care
Before it is too late and there is no time

She is the Goddess
You may not know now
You are lucky to have her
And this you will not realise now

Mother will never think ill
No matter how is her child
In every possibility she helps
In whatever difficulties may be her child

## 17. Memories

My heart is full of memories
Memories that are given by you
They seem sweet sometimes
And also bring me the thought about you

It's not so easy as you think
To forget and never look at you
You have gone a bit far
But in my heart there is still some part of you

There are so many things we did support
You are always there in my mind
But now you are not there for my support
You are like my breath, you are my life

Without you I am a non-living thing
There is no way I can forget you my dear
You are the best thing that ever happened to me
Life is unpredictable which seperated is from each other

You are my world
You are like a God to me
You are my everything
You are the life support system for me

It's not easy to express my feelings
And my gratitude to you
Now I don't have much strength
That I can express my feelings to you

# 18. Wind

Wind is very important to us
But sometimes very dangerous also
It has some positive points
And some negative also

Breeze can be considered good
As it is associated with romance
It makes the person more attractive
And builds up the romance

Wind is needed to cool down the place
To give relief to us from the scorching heat
It is good for our health also
As it freshens up our skin

Wind in the form of tornado
Can uproot the houses easily also
Takes away a lot of life
From plants to animals to humans

Wind carry a lot of disease with it
It can spread any epidemic
It may make the life of slumps
A very big endemic

Wind may bring dust and sand dunes
It may bring various troubles
It is the part and parcel of life
It makes us closer to nature's troubles

## 19. Caste and Reservation

When will India think over the castes
Creed, sex, religion, status, and wealth
The day when she comes over this
It will improve in its physical health

When you go to the college you understand
Marks are not that important if you are the lower class
You have the reservation of seats
And with a lower marks you get the desired class

In competitive exams
My select the most deserving candidates
But if you are a so called "backward class"
You get an upper hand among the candidates

For the backward class
50% marks are enough sometimes
But the things are different for the higher category
90% marks are not enough sometimes

Be it engineering, medical, or any other intellectual profession
Marks are not the better option to get
The lower the caste, the better it
It's certificate is the best option to get

This is the land which wants to progress
This is the land which is developing in its task
There is an irony in this fact
As everyone is trying to be in the backward class

Her economy is blooming
It is touching the sky
Even the population of backward people
Is about to touch the sky

In the country everyone wants to be backward
Everyone wants to fight to get the certificate
The country that gives reservation in every category
One day General class will be requiring a minority certificate

## 20. Changes

Change is the only constant
Changes has to be there always
We need to change for better future
The orthodox policies need to change always

The things which were crime then
May become the new trend now
The law needs to be changed
And the crime should be nullified somehow

Change has to be there
Sometimes to incorporate the change in thought
What you think to be bad
May have now become a common thought

Trends in fashion changes every minute
We need to accept these changes also
The new things which were not accepted before
Are needed to be accepted also

Time changes as generations change
Due to change in technology our gadgets change
We need to learn these new things
Otherwise our status doesn't change

Languages have also changed
Whether it be English or Hindi
There is American English
And many new alphabets in Hindi

Do not be a fool my friend
For our betterment accept these changes
As our ancestors accepted the changes we made
Let our new generation also make some changes

## 22. Be Careful

The world is dual Jaeed
You will never see the other one
It is hidden beneath the Sun
It is to be hidden so it never confronts anyone

The love may be shown
But the hatred overshadows
The care may be there
But you may not see the cause that it bothers

There is always a flip side
We need to look at it
The world is manipulative
It will show the things that is for you, fit

You can never see underneath the mind
The evil that is living
The things always look beautifully presented
But beware of the pack overshadowing

Trust the trusted but not always
They may be the one to stab your back for their gain
Beware of such things that may cause
You not to trust anyone again

Carefully you need to walk
In this path of life
You will never know who is your friend
And who is that enemy of life

Now it doesn't mean
That we be afraid of everyone
There are only few serpents
There are friends that are very helpful ones

Identify those fiends of your's
I know it is difficult to do that
Time teaches us everything
How to come out of such a hat

Believe in your dreams always
At least take risk for them
The frenemies will come as an obstacle
You need to move ahead identifying them

## 23. Good Bye

It is time to say goodbye
I am starting a new chapter of life
Life changes with time
We need to accept them always

I have gathered a lot of memories
I am leaving behind a lot of friends
Everyone had been so good to me
And helping me to cope up always

I have grown up wiser here
Learning something from all of you
Not only my colleagues but also my students
They had some knowledge in store too

I am going from here
With a new level of maturity
Everyone has been so supportive
And had trusted me with responsibility

I have joked with friends
Got angry sometimes
Handled situations with maturity
And like a child sometimes

I have a lot to say about everyone
The dictionary will not be enough
I will waste a lot of time
Because the things done by you are more than enough

I was lucky enough to work with you all
I get a mother, brother, sister, father here
There was a home-like feeling here for me
I have got many friends here

I have always learnt from all of you
Will never ever forget your teaching
I will always be obliged to you all
For all the things you have taught me

I will miss each and everyone of you
You all have a special place in my heart
But this is the time which comes in everyone's life
The time when we need to part

## 24. It is easy

It is easy to be a man
You just have to think of your future
It is easy to be a man
You will be the one on whom the family will depend on future

It is easy to be a man
Hitting a Woman should not be in your nature
It is easy to be a man
You cannot get hit by a woman either

It is easy to be a man
You are a molester for every stranger
It is easy to be a man
You cannot talk to a girl who is a stranger

It is easy to be a man
You are judged by the amount you earn
It is easy to be a man
You cannot get offended by a girl's look at every turn

It is easy to be a man
You are expected to be strong always
It is easy to be a man
You have to respect the other gender in any way

# 25. Emotional Poem

I wonder why all the poems which are emotional
Touch your internal heart and make you cry
I wonder how come everyone can relate to it
Even if they have never fallen in love and still cry

The emotions that they have are very sensitive
It has all the pain that you cannot think of
I wonder why you cannot forget the emotion
And the poem forces you to have someone to think of

The whole life seems to come around the same thing
And we just think of the emotional poems
I wonder how do they change our feelings
And it's none like other poems

Emotional poems are intense and in depth
They make you wonder through your life
I wonder how can people read or write such things
Without thinking of their past life!!!

# 26. Smiling Face

Smiling face is always deceiving
There may be a hidden pain in it
You may not know what is the thing
Which has caused the severe pain indeed

The tears hide behind the laughter
Smiling pain is dreadful indeed
The life is very miserable when this is the case
We are deceiving not the world but ourselves indeed

There is fear of mockery from others
Which may stop you from showing your feelings
Sometimes there may be love for them
Which doesn't want to show them your feelings

You may feel bad within
You may fall in guilt trap
The pain is unbearable sometimes
But you need to keep the emotions trapped

The tears come out
When you are totally alone
When you are in the crowd aloof
Or when you are listening to a song

What is the whole situation
Is totally alone and not known
The crowd doesn't bother your aloofness
It's like all the song which are sung

Why is it this way no one knows
You may be sad but may not know the reason
There is the time when you are totally low
Whether it may not be the sad season

No one wants to show their feelings
But the loved ones come to know of it
They sometimes are able to help you
But sometimes they can only feel pity for it

Melancholy is just not a feeling
It can destroy ones inner peace completely
It's best friend tension creeps in
Increasing the sadness completely

You are trapped in a vicious circle
You can never come out of it
The peace is gone and small things make you sad
Mental torture and feeling of disgust together with you sit

Crying silently or not letting out the grief
You are killing yourself slowly
We need to share such feelings to someone
Don't disguise the feeling completely

## 27. Melancholy

Sometimes you are alone and lonely
Sometimes you just feel that way
Some Days we don't have anyone to talk to
Some Days we don't want to talk in any way

We may not be lonely when alone
But feel lonely in the crowd
It is a very compulsive feeling
Which is not at all bound

The friends near you are dear to you
But still you don't want to talk to them
They may get the negative vibes from you
But still in no way can the space be filled by them

They try their best to cheer you up
But nothing at all seems to work
You become more lonely and want to leave
But you can't as it is a social protocol

The pain is very much hidden in your heart
You cannot pronounce it to anyone
The well wishers come to know of it
But the loneliness can be fixed by no one

You are always perplexed on such situation
You don't know why you feel like that
When asked you have no answer
No reason to stick to the melancholy bait

Your feeling is anonymous
The origin is never known
You feel like Antonio sometimes
And in all such situation

It is not you don't want to share your feeling
It may take your friends apart
Understanding might get rusted
Tearing the flesh of this relationship apart

But still somehow
The friend cope up with you
They know they can't do anything else
So they try to console you

Melancholy comes unnoticed
It goes without bidding you farewell
But you have to know how to hide it
As you may be throwing someone's happiness in the well

# 28. Destiny of Life

Life is not what it looks like
It will change every moment
You will not know when the good days come
As it can knock at your door any moment

You may be confused
Why is your life in such a misery
Worry a lot and be tensed always
Not knowing when will you get your treasury

Time will come
You will get what you want
Have patience every time
Dont right away jump to conclusion

Waiting for a right time is good
Waiting too long is not
Sometimes you have to know
That was not your path

Don't just stick around to one thing
You need to change the path
You may not be destined to do that
You will may be prosper in another cart

You find many people in life
Many will stick along with you
Many will part from you
Many will become a stranger for you

These are the matter of life
They have to happen
You need to always walk in life
With a full proof backup plan

Plan A may not work
Make Plan B your A
Now you need to think of another plan as well
So that no one in your life has a say

You never know your destiny
You can just plan your way
Sometimes the path needs to be changed
But the destination remains there

# 29. Big Dream

I want to do something big
And something great indeed
I want to achieve what I have aspired
I want to live my dream

It seems confusing to me
It seems very difficult now
I have been in a different sector
So it seems out of reach now

It has to be started from scratch
And that is difficult it seems
You know studying ABC is difficult
But novels are easy to read

Life has taken a complete turn
What I was planning doesn't work it seems
I had come here with a plan
All are now shattering apart it seems

I am lost right now, but have not lost my hope
Hope is the thing which keeps me going
I have to work and achieve it
Change of plans is what I will be needing

## 30. Feeling... Let it GO!!!

It is very difficult to hide your feelings
Whether it is happy or sad
Sometimes we need to just relax
And let go of our emotions apart

When you are happy
Let the whole world know of it
Let them be jealous of you
And show every feeling that there is

You may not get the next time to celebrate
As happiness don't last for long
So celebrate the moment to its fullest
Just dance along and sing a song

You can never miss this chance
Yell out to the world that you are happy
Cherish every that you have got
Be happier with as the time passes by

When you are sad
Don't let your feeling to be overshadowed
Let out your grief also
As it will kill you from inside every moment

Tell it to your best friend
Write it somewhere and let it go
You can even type it in facebook
You will get some relief, you know.

When you are filled with anxiety
Burst out at someone close
You will feel good in a moment
And you will feel better again

When you are angry
Don't keep it in your heart
Let it out my friend
Otherwise it will tear you apart

So whatever feeling it may be
They should not last for long
You need to live your life
Like a merry making song

# 31. Introvert

It takes me time to be close to people
I can't just let out my feelings at once
I don't talk much sometimes as I am reserved
Sometimes it's hard to stop me from my talk

I only talk when it is absolutely necessary
But sometimes I blabber out anything
The things that I say makes some sense
But sometimes you don't find sense in anything

I like to talk to myself as well
I do it lot more than you think
It may not be that I am talking about you
It may be sometimes the things I link

I take time to come back from emotions
My mood sometimes change immediately
I may be angry the whole day for no reason
Sometimes the emotions disappear suddenly

I can laugh at some serious moments
I can cry in lone during the happy times
My expressions don't depend on the occasion
It depends on my mood at that time

I don't believe in showing my emotions
I overshadow it very quickly
I may laugh but be sad from inside
I may sublime my anger quickly

I can't actually express my feelings easily
I am afraid of being mocked or felt pity for
I don't know why do I feel in such a way
No one has ever done these things before

## 32. Path You Choose

The path you choose is decided by you
No one else chooses it for
The path may seem beautiful first
But dangers come after followed by you

There are always the places
Where you think your path is wrong
But it takes time to adjust my friend
Just go with the rhythm of the song

The path that has been chosen
May be after a lot of analysis done by you
You had seen the pros and cons
So don't be afraid and just follow as it was chosen by you

There are always the loop hole in your thought
So don't worry for your mistakes done
They are the ones to let you grow
Just try to improve them and move on

You need to try
Try hard for your chosen path
There is always something fruitful in it
You just need to find that

It is not always you are right
Your chosen path may be not what you might have thought
Just don't worry, it's never to late
You can always take a different path.

In order to grow, changes are needed
In order to change, risks are to be taken
In order to take risk, you need to change path
In order to change path, you need to awaken

Just believe in yourself
Just live up your dreams
The path is never filled with roses
It is not like what it seems

Always remember one important thing
Other's plate are always better than yours
Now its your concepts that lets you grow
Or makes you to take risk and make it yours

Never be satisfied with what you have
Always aspire for more
If you want to be successful
You need to come out of your comfort zone.

## 33. Everyone is Talented

Everyone is talented
In some ways or other
Your talent may be surprisingly different
Which may seem unlikely for others

Talent is not limited to song, dance or arts
To act, to mimic or to write
It has a very wide range of things
Which may not be at your sight.

Loving someone is a tallent
You need to love everyone
As everyone don't get love
So your lovely presence will cheer them up

Making someone sad happy
Is the greatest talent in this world
You have made them forget their melancholy
And led them to a happy world

Making instant jokes is also a talent
Everyone cannot do that
You are the hilarious one
And you should be proud of that

Cooking is a talent
It feeds when you are hungry
You can cook for poor and distribute
Or even cook making people happy in your family

Talking without thinking is also a talent
As you can let out your feelings easily
You are never reserved
You can make friends very easily

Taking stress happily is also a talent
Not everyone can do that
You are blessed as you can come out of it so easily
When others are struggling to do that

You are talented if you can take care of your family
You are talented if you are always there for someone
You are talented if you can talk calmly
You are talented if you don't judge people

Don't feel inferior my friend
Thinking that you are not talented
There is always some talent in you
That you are not being able to state

## 34. Miss You Always

The life is always not fair
You don't get what you want the most
There is always a place which is untouched
You are lost and your thoughts are gone

I still miss you so much
You are always irreplaceable
You were the one in my life
You were the only one reliable

I love you
Have always loved you
I know I cannot repay you back now
There is an empty place in my heart for you

I used to laugh with you
We used to have so much of fun
You were the enjoyment provider for me
You were the real one

The day you left me
I still try to find you
When I have nowhere to go
My eyes just search for you

I know you are gone
Gone far away from me
You will never return now
But I still want you with me

My love was not enough it seems
God loved you more than me
He wanted you at any cost
So he just snatched you from me

I know you are not there
But sometimes I feel your presence
I know it is just my hallucination
But I just can't cope up with your absence

I fake my laugh for others
I am really sad within
I have to say you were my life
Now I am just a dead body with soul within

I regret that I was unable to do for you
I wanted to give you all the happiness that you were craving for
I just don't know why it happened
May be I had done a lot of sin before

I miss your love, your care and concern
Your advices were always there
I miss the talk that we share
I want to say you a lot but now you are not there

## 35. Live up to You

When you choose something
You choose it for its pros
But when you are doing it
The cons are seen more than pros

You just need to keep doing it
As you always had aspired
You should in no way leave the work
And call yourself later a coward

The thing you have chosen is always right
If not you have to make it right
You cannot change the plan so often
You have to now see the side that is bright

As you chose it for your betterment
You now need to make it your cult
You should not give up your dream so easily
Just because it was difficult

Try try and try
You will surely succeed
Always remember one thing
Life has to be difficult when you want to succeed

Love you life as you use to before
Never ever think of cursing it
It has been gifted it to you
Just don't make worse of it

You need to look at your work
As a top supreme
Then only you will be able to work
And make your life supreme

Hardwork is key to success
It just doesn't come as a God's gift
You need to do the difficult work
In order to have your life to lift

Praise your work
As no one else will do it for you
Then you will start enjoying it
And life will become easy for you

Face everyday like a challenge
Then you will not get bored
Challenge yourself to the utmost
Then you will see you have always scored

## 36. Will You be There...

If I am not able to sleep
Will you sing a lullaby for me?
If I am unable to wake up
Will you become an alarm clock for me?
If I am not able to eat
Will you become the medicine for it?
If I eat too much
Will you be the reason for it?
If I want to eat but don't have food
Will you be the one to cook for me?
If I have too much to eat
Will you be there to share it with me?
If I want a friend to talk with
Will you do that for me too?
If I am filled with anger
Will you let me pour it out on you?
If I want to cry
Will you provide the shoulder to me?
If I want to laugh
Will you be the reason for me?
If I want to tell a horrible joke
Will you laugh at it?
If I want to tell you all of my truth
Will you in your heart, keep it?
If I want to dance

Will you pair up with me?
If I want to sing
Will you tolerate it for me?
If I am depressed
Will you cheer me up?
If I am lonely and forgotten
Will you make it up?
If I want die
Will you be there to bury me?
Tell me one thing
Will you share these things with me?

# 37. Hope is the Mantra

Hope is the thing
That rules the world
It is that feeling
Which helps to live in this world

Whatever you do
Always hope for the best
If you do not hope for it, who else will
You need to keep the judgement best

If you are failing
Don't ever lose your hope
The day will come when you will shine
It will help you to cope

If you are successful indeed
Keep your hopes always up
You will be able to grow only then
You will everyday have a chance to grow up

The light of hope should never die
It burns till you want it to
You need to have faith in yourself
And then your hope will live upto you

Trying is the mantra here
You need to try always
You should not feel hopeless anytime
The light needs to be kindled always

Your hope can kindle someone else's hope
You need to have such a flame in your thought
Never give up on anything that you aspire of
Just let the light strong enough

## 38. Enjoy Every Moment

We need to enjoy everyday
We need to cherish every moment
To make our life happy
We need to relive every moment

There are some special unforgettable days
These are very special indeed
You enjoy every bit of that moment
These days are always remembered indeed

Life never gives you a second chance
Live it, love it, enjoy it, every time
Forget about every other anxiety
Just make every moment to be remembered every time

The trips we go with friends
Are one of those feelings in fact
You cherish your bonding and come close
Every moment lived is kept intact.

You overcome your fears with friends
You do the things that were never done
You find your inner self through it
Spiritually and Mentally you are once more born

Life is full of struggle
In order to do this you need to take a break
Break is always needed for our betterment
It refreshes our soul in every take.

You become as pure and live as the Ganga
You find the inner peace of your soul
You rejuvenate the life you have lived
And come closer to your bonds.

The merry making, the social gathering
The playful times indeed
The whole moment you live in your break
Is only yours indeed

You fall in love again with yourself
You are energised again
You at every moment are there in its hangover
You want to live that moment again and again

Such moments need to come every now and then
You need to make it possible somehow
You will be happy after it
And forget all your grief, at least for that moment, anyhow.

# 39. Dream of the Soul

We all have a dream
They may not come true
The purity of thought lies in each
They are really very hard to get through

The soul's dreams are really
Very difficult to achieve
It is very pure
Purer than the Ganga indeed

The soul cherises its beauty
The beauty it is drenched with
It's dreams are not that simple
They are complicated but sweet

The soul wants to cherish
Every moment lived
The soul wants to relive them
If they were fruitfully lived

It dreams to reach to the top
Higher than any other being
It wants to achieve everything
That can be achieved in this universe indeed

Love is what it wants
From everyone around it
Faith is what it desires
From all the souls around it

Trust is the thing
Which it feeds upon
Friendship is the beauty
Which keeps its purity on

Soul wants all these
But doesn't know how to get them
It is inactive till you are not active
You have to help it in order to achieve them

The dreams are complicated
Only till you don't rejuvenate the soul
You need to be careful with it
To cherish the dream of the soul

# 40. Mistakes not Repeated

Sometimes you don't know your mistakes
That made you to be treated that way
You are confused with that treatment
And you don't know what to say

You are lost deep in your thought
You don't know how to get out of it
You still try to find the way out
But you are still stuck at it

The reason is quite small for you
But it might have made a grave impact
Your apologies won't help
As it has torn the loved ones heart apart

There is a feeling of guilt in you
Your true nature is not found
You are shattered by now
You are alone even when everyone is around

You are still not sure
How has that thing affected the person you love
But sometimes you have to live up to
The expectation of the person you love

Some mistakes can be forgotten
Some are bound to create enmity
They are sometimes not that big for you
But you have lost the tranquillity

You try your best
To make things right
Your efforts are not enough
You have lost your far sight

Don't give up my friend
Things will become right again
Your mistakes will be forgiven once more
The relationship will bond again

# 41. Life... A Teacher

Life is a greatest teacher
It teaches you everything
It is the one that guides you
And make you the best indeed

You may not know
What may come up to you
That essense of surprise
Is what makes sense for you

You will learn something new always
As the train moves on
The journey is full of adventure
And you don't know what stations may come

Live everyday to the fullest
Make the best of every moment
You need to have some memories
For each and every moment

It teaches you how to enjoy
How to judge people in the best way
You come to know of your true partners
The true faces of people in your way

It makes your judgement clear
What is right or wrong for you
It teaches you through trial and error
Or from others' experience who are close to you

Life is sometimes cruel
Sometimes sweeter than the flower
But it is the greatest teacher
Better than any other

Don't be afraid my friend
Always take risk and gamble with your life
You don't know what knowledge it has instored
That will make for you an amazing life

# 42. Unknown Cause of Feeling

I am feeling low today
But I am unaware of the cause of it
It is quite surprisingly different
I normally do know the reason for it.

I want to cry, cry out loud
Tears want to roll down my eyes
I am trying to control them
But my efforts are burdening my eyes.

I am too emotional it seems
What are the worldly matters affecting me
I have asked my heart so many times
But it is also not being able to answer me.

I am sad, I know it very well
I want to shed tears
There are no personal grief that bothers me
But still my feelings are like that.

I have nothing to grief upon
There are no reason on my side
I fear that if I let go of these emotions
People may think otherwise.

There was a time
When I used to cry at slightest of pain
But now the things have changed
I cannot even tell my grief at my utmost pain.

I don't want anyone to know it
I don't want anyone to be bothered by it
I want to keep it to myself nowadays
I just want to live, burdened with it.

Today the things are different
I don't know the reason for my sadness
I am trying to laugh at slightest things
But that is not able to control my coldness.

I am very confused
I am losing my hope it seems
I don't know what is happening
I am trying to smile, but it's very hard, it seems.

My sad face seems to affect some people
I am trying to cover it up with a smile
But the things are not working that way
I have not made them believe even for a while.

You may tell that it is because I miss my mom
But I do miss her everyday
That is not the reason I know very well
Otherwise I will be sad for the whole day.

You may tell that as my plans are not working
The way it was planned

That I feel is vague
As I am doing my Plan B instead.

There can be many reasons
That you can think of
But the reasons are not sufficient
As the reason I cannot think of.

# 43. I Admire You

You know the fact I always want
That you are always there for me
You are near me always
That you always talk to me

You feel like the reason for my life
You make my heart beat fast
Your sight takes away my breath
In my mind your smell ever lasts

You give me courage, You give me hope
You are the one who gives me strength
You are my life, you are my soul
You are the cause of my good health

I wake up every morning
To just have a sight of you
I just can't sleep at night
Until I don't talk to you

You are innocent that's what I like
You are good enough for anyone
You can't control your emotions and its wonderful
You can never hide your feelings for anyone

You try, try your best
To become a star in everyone's life
But you forget to shine for yourself
You never think of your life

You are emotionally attached
You love every human being
You are great which you don't know of
Your humility is what I am admiring

# 44. Changing Friendship

I have forgotten someone
Someone else has forgotten me
I have not talked with someone
Someone else is not talking to me

This is always the case with everyone
'Keep in touch' are just mere words after all
It means a lot to someone
But someone else is not bothered at all

Once you depart, you part your ways
Your love is overshadowed but is there
You don't have time always now
To whom you promised you will always be there

You want to keep that promise
But now you are busy with other promises
You sometimes feel guilty
But sometimes you forget those promises

As you didn't keep your promise
Someone else is doing the same unknowingly
You always try to bridge the gap made
But then again increase it unwillingly

But you are also lonely
You start questioning your friendship
You start remembering the days
And those now give you hardship

New friends take the place of old ones
As old ones remain in our heart only
Change is the only constant in fact
And now we create a vicious circle repeatedly

# 45. Plan

I want to try out some new things
But I fear from them being successful or not
There is a high risk involved in it
There are a lot of things to be considered which are not

It needs a lot of analysis
Even though it seems to be finished
I have to think of other plans
Before this plan can be executed

I don't know whether I will be able to do it
Whether it is the correct thing to be done
I have to make up my mind
And do the things that were left undone

Sometimes it seems quite difficult
Sometimes it is as easy as making a shake
Sometimes it seems legitimate
Sometimes it is the worst possible mistake

I am confused
Don't know which direction to move
I want to clarify my thoughts
And then only will I be able to move

For this I have to let go
Of all the relations I am in
I may even have to break some
And distribute all the pain

It's a very risky process
I need more experience for it
I am trying best to gain them
But all seems to be less indeed

Sometimes I feel I won't be able to do it
Sometimes I feel not to give it up
I just hope that my plans work
As I will try my best not to give up

# 46. Memory Lane

I talked to very few people in my primary
Only few were known to me
We were friends then very close indeed
Now they are just memories for me

We played in our school fearlessly
We enjoyed every time indeed
We now have gone far apart with school change
Now you are in my memories indeed

New school was big, managed to get friends
Friends changed so did friendship
Many came many went in the journey
There are now memories left of those things

We grew together to be men
We had a seperate bonding in fact
We were special for each other
Now the moments are in memories in tact

We had to follow our dreams
Change our course of action
Got seperated to cherish our themes
To build more memory attraction

College days are beautiful in every way
Many new friends joined the path
Old friends got lost now
Somewhere forgotten in the memory lane

Different sort of memories were building
A long lasting friendship was thriving
A dream never to be forgotten
All the moments were amazingly arriving

Sequence of three years passed in no time
Building beautiful friendship in it
All emotions, all closeness and all promises
Are now left in the memory lane

The group travels have ended
The group celebrations are not there
All the fun that we had
Are lost in the memory lair

We grow, move away, start working indeed
Increasing our friend circle
Now friends have fun working with you
You are in a place where you have to fit in the circle

These friends are also lost
When you go away from them
All the things you do together
Are with you in you memory lane

# 47. Phobia

I am afraid to talk to female stranger
Not because I am an introvert
But with the opinion that I will be judged
No matter what explanation is given it won't be accepted

I am reluctant to offer food to strangers
Not because I don't want to
But as people will take it differently
They may take it to be poison or so

I feel scared to stand in a crowd
Not because I have a phobia
But it is so because anything can happen
And that strange feeling is a phobia

I feel not right to help strangers
Not because I cannot help them
But I am afraid of only one fact
That there may be a criminal hidden within them

I want to offer sweets to all the kids
Play with them or get lost in their innocence
But I am afraid to do so
As I may be taken for other instance

I know the world is free
It is safe for me
But somethings I am afraid to do
For some reasons known to you and me

# 48. Questions

I have some question in my mind
Why is life so adventurous?
Why don't the plans work in the way they should?
Why are we not able to cope up with a few things?

It seems difficult to change
Even though we know that it is necessary
We want to stay as we want
Even though it has become a fictitious accessory

You know things will change
But you feel sad when someone is after you
You are lost at times
But have no ways that you need to be

You want everyone to be good to you
To always appreciate you for your doings
But there is no improvement
If you are not criticised for your workings

You want life to be adventurous
But you are afraid of ups and down
You want it to be amazing
But you are afraid of turmoils to come

You want to fall in love
But you are afraid of relationships
You want to all the things
But are afraid of the social well beings

You want to be the king
But don't want to struggle for it
You want to be healthy
But don't want to work for it

We want everything in the platter
But that is not possible
We need to work hard to achieve
But that becomes impossible

## 49. Be Happy

Happiness needs to be shared
It is that feeling which overshadows everything
It should not be hidden
It should be the part of everything

When you are happy
Let the whole world know of it
Spread it whatever be the circumstance
You are happy so let the world know it

Your smile may make a difference
May make someone else forget of his worries
You will see that people become happy
And they will be able to see their trophies

We are happy in a rare circumstance
We are mostly thinking of our troubles
So we need to show it fully
We need to burst out the sad bubbles

Even if you have a grave problem
Just handle it with a smile
You may not know you will feel great
And let you go on for a couple of more mile

Your smile does not always mean
You are hiding your grief
It sometimes means
That you can handle that thief

When you are feeling low
Try to smile and see the difference
Your lowness will disappear
And you will be in happy confluence

I know it is difficult to do
But at least we can try it
Smile need very less muscles
But frowning needs multiples of it

Smile always
And that is the mantra
It will relief others near you
And you will see a difference in every encounter

## 50. Teaching, A Profession

Teaching is a very respectful profession
It is one of the difficult one as well
A teacher encompasses continual learning
And imparts his teaching as well

This profession helps to create others
Building a society bestows on it
The values imparted are what is carried forward
The wellbeing of others depends on it

A teacher modules the life of the person
He is the one who teaches what is right or wrong
He helps anyone without any consideration
Without thinking what he will be paid on

There is a very high position for him
He needs to stay away from any prejudicial thinking
He is the guiding light for his students
And helps them to think beyond anyone's thinking

A teacher cares for his students
Cherishes their successful deeds
Motivates them at every failure
And mentors them when there is a need